Practical Ideas for Kitchens and Bathrooms

LOFT

Editorial Coordination: Cristina Paredes
Texts: Sandra Moya
Editor: Cristian Campos
Translation: Matthew Clarke
Art Director: Mireia Casanovas Soley
Layout: Anabel Naranjo

Editorial project:

2007 © **LOFT Publications**
Via Laietana 32, 4° Of. 92
08003 Barcelona, Spain
Tel.: +34 932 688 088
Fax: +34 932 687 073
loft@loftpublications.com
www.loftpublications.com

ISBN: 978-84-95832-74-0

Printed in China

If you would like to propose works to include in our upcoming books, please
email us at loft@loftpublications.com.

In some cases it has been impossible to locate copyright owners of the images
published in this book. Please contact the publisher if you are the copyright
owner of any of the images published here.

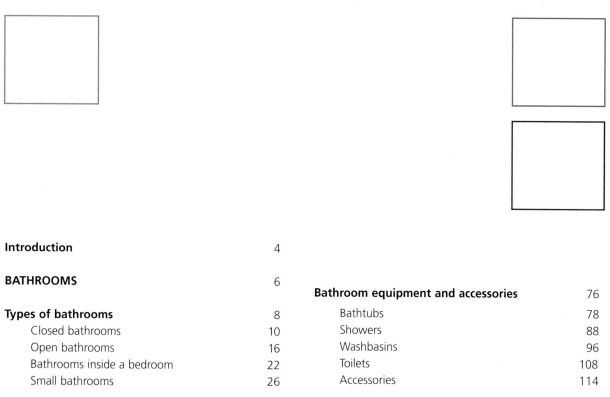

Bathrooms have undergone a complete transformation over the course of history by evolving along with the customs and characteristics of each era and culture. In ancient times, taking a bath was synonymous with ritual, a cult of the body and even, in public bathhouses, meeting friends. In other periods, hygiene was not exactly a priority, so bathing facilities were virtually non-existent or had no fixed place in a home. For decades, toilet amenities and bathtubs were moved from room to room as required. The 19th century saw an increasing concern for hygiene and so bathrooms began to be set up in a self-contained space that was considered as an entity separate from the rest of the home. Technological advances have led to new models and materials, as well as cladding that is more resistant to water. Bathrooms are now chosen with decorative criteria, and they have gradually gained prominence as a space for hygiene and relaxation. Bathrooms can be designed as big spaces filled with light and divided into clearly delimited areas, or as small rooms with highly prac-

tical means of taking full advantage of the space, so that users can benefit from their functional purpose while also using them to relax and rest—all this without forsaking the privacy that is particularly necessary in this room. The latest designs opt for a combination of traditional materials (wood, glass, tiles and marble) and innovative, highly resistant cladding that is easy to maintain (porcelain, resins...), without neglecting the latest technological breakthroughs in toilets and general installations, such as the application of domotics. The designs currently on offer make it possible to create a bathroom that is classical or state-of-the-art, rustic or minimalist, with a look at the past or an empathy with cutting-edge styles. The idea of the bathroom as a space in which health is combined with relaxation is largely derived from Scandinavia and Japan. New accessories and details add personality to a bathroom and take it far beyond its functional use. Bathrooms have adapted to today's exacting requirements to become a small haven of peace and privacy.

The concept of the kitchen has evolved with the passing of time. At the beginning of the 20th century it was a neglected room, relegated to a secondary plane and never shown to outsiders. The kitchen was exclusively reserved for cooks and servants, even in quite modest houses. It only served for the end result of its activity, i.e., for preparing the dishes that were served in the dining room, but nobody worried about how this room was organized and what it looked like. Servants gradually started disappearing from homes and women had to replace them and take on their domestic chores, but the kitchen continued to occupy the most isolated area in the house. Domestic machines emerged with the intention of liberating women from the hard work involved in running a home, although, in practice, they only increased the number of activities that women had to control: the new advances meant that there were more clothes to wash and more dishes to prepare. The woman's role only changed when she decided to abandon purely domestic chores and seek work outside the house. With the new technological advances that have been made over the years, the kitchen has opened up to the rest of the house to become a practical space filled with light.

The gradual disappearance of the dining room as the family meeting place and the greater emphasis on comfort has made the kitchen the most important space in the house, used not only for preparing food but also for gathering together the family. It now fulfils the role of the living room in the 18th and 19th centuries—the place where visitors to the house are received. More time is now taken to choose the materials and decoration for a kitchen, it is allocated more space and a wide range of practical ideas are exploited to increase its capacity and make its organization more efficient. The new concept of the kitchen assigns each of its tasks to a different area. In this way, every zone can be used in comfort while a space is reserved for gatherings and meals. All today's kitchen designs favor bright, comfortable spaces where preparing food and sitting down to eat become a real pleasure.

Bathrooms

Types of bathrooms
Styles, materials, lighting, and color
Bathroom equipment and accessories

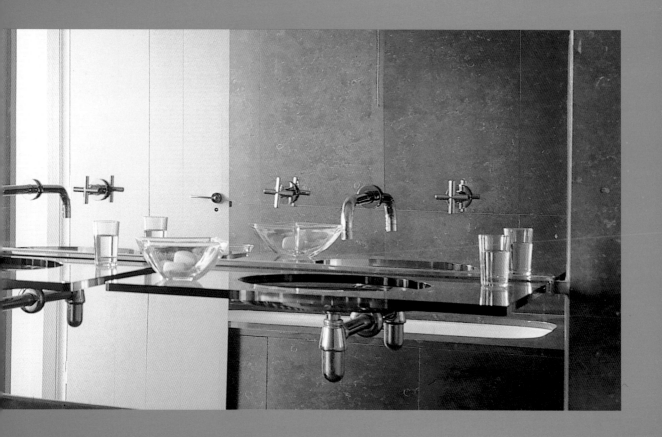

Types of bathrooms

In recent years, the bathroom has acquired a prominence that it did not enjoy even a decade ago. It is no longer just a space devoted to personal hygiene: thanks to the modern trends in interior design, the idea of a bathroom as a space for relaxing and resting has become increasingly popular. According to these trends, the bathroom should become an intimate space in which we can allow ourselves to withdraw and enjoy a moment of privacy and relaxation. And all this has been achieved without renouncing comfort. The dimensions of your bathroom do not matter, because these days the combination of traditional materials (wood, glass, tiles) and more innovative ones (porcelain, stone, aluminum) make possible all types of decorative solutions.

Closed bathrooms

Open bathrooms

© Joy von Tiedemann

Bathrooms inside a bedroom

Small bathrooms

Closed bathrooms

Installing a bathroom in an enclosed space makes it possible to isolate it from the other rooms in the home and turn it into that relaxing space that we need at the end of the day. The type of furniture that you add or the way you distribute the space will depend on your requirements and the number of people that are going to use the bathroom.

Glass is one of the materials most suited to bathrooms with no good source of natural light. The type of glass—transparent or opaque—and its decoration—smooth or with some kind of motif—depends on your taste, but there are two factors that you should bear in mind. If you want to create an intimate setting, the ideal solution is opaque glass. However, transparent glass will provide you with much greater depth and make the bathroom look bigger. Furthermore, made-to-measure furniture will help you to take maximum advantage of the space.

© Eugeni Pons

A washbasin, a toilet and a shower or bathtub are the main elements of this type of bathroom.

© Kirsty Kriegel

© Mitsuo Matsuoka

© José Luis Hausmann

© Joshua McHugh

© Joshua McHugh

© Eugeni Pons

Open bathrooms

Until just a few years ago, the idea of an open bathroom was unconventional and, in fact, almost unimaginable. Fortunately, the latest design trends have enabled the traditional concept to evolve to the point of embracing this type of bathroom. The decision to create an open bathroom depends on the personal tastes of the home owner—not everybody wants spaces with no boundaries or visual barriers. Nowadays, many people opt to live in a loft, which is usually a large living area with open spaces and no interior walls. It is in this type of home that more and more open bathrooms are gradually being installed.

An open bathroom is usually small in size and, above all, very functional. For this reason, the design of bathroom equipment has become ever more ingenious, original and modern. Elements that once went unnoticed no longer fall outside the limits of design.

Taking maximum advantage of the space is fundamental, as is taking care of the details that will endow your bathroom with personality.

© Luis Asín

© Eduardo Consuegra

© Bruno Klomfar

Square, rectangular and round washbasins are gradually taking over from the classic oval models.

A combination of different styles in a single room reflects the personality of the home's occupant.

NO

- To a parquet floor especially treated to prevent damp.
- To faucets with a cutting-edge design in combination with a marble washbasin.

YES

- To parquet and the sense of warmth that it provides.
- To porcelain, glass and wood washbasins with modern faucets.
- To pale-colored tiles on the walls, as they enhance luminosity.

Bathrooms inside a bedroom

A bathroom should be an extremely functional space. In this case, the aim is to create a practical, comfortable room for two people. The most important thing is to find the most appropriate layout, which partly depends on the size of the room. In general, this type of bathroom has an L or U shape, which makes it possible to install a washbasin, bathroom or shower and toilet, while taking full advantage of the space available. In this respect, one of the most original and increasingly popular options is installing a washbasin that incorporates a faucet unit embedded in its top.

Lighting is another basic element when it comes to decorating a bathroom. The selection of materials will depend on the availability or otherwise of natural light. The installation of halogen lamps above the mirror is almost obligatory, as this avoids undesirable shadows. It should also be remembered that the choice of material for a bathroom partition will also determine the amount of light that enters the space.

In bathrooms with no windows, general light sources should be used to create a clean, bright light.

© Joy von Tiedemann

© Eduardo Consuegra, Pablo Rojas

© Alfonso Postigo

© Alfonsþ Postigo

© Nuria Fuentes

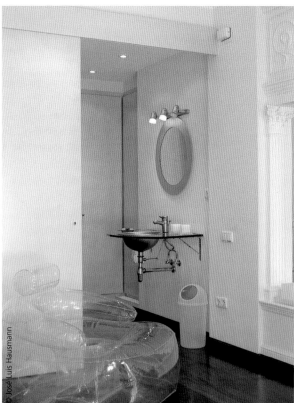

Small bathrooms

athrooms in modern homes tend to be small, and this factor only heightens the importance of their decoration. Practical solutions are required to take full advantage of the space and achieve a functional layout. Sometimes it may not be possible to obtain the layout you wanted because a piece of furniture (e.g. a closet) does not fit. However, it is not only the furniture that is important—the small details will also help to provide the desired sense of spaciousness. It is vital to try to avoid dead spaces in the corners, in order to exploit the maximum possibilities of the bathroom.

It is essential to decide what elements are really needed: there is no sense in installing a bidet if the size or configuration of the bathroom does not allow it; neither is it a good idea to put in a bathtub instead of a shower when space is very limited. Remember that it is best to opt for pale-colored furniture in a small bathroom. Aluminum and glass also contribute a sense of spaciousness.

In small spaces, walls painted or clad in a pale color will help to create a brighter setting.

© José Luis Hausmann

© Sergio Mah

NO

• To dark colors on walls, because they make the room look smaller and colder.

• To unnecessary closets and equipment, because they would reduce the room's functionality and restrict its space.

YES

• To small mirrors with a frame, to set up a visual contrast with the bathroom equipment.

• To tiles in the shower area, as they are designed to resist contact with water.

• To halogen lamps on the mirror, as they produce a clean light with no shadows.

• To an insulation system that maintains the pleasant temperature of a small bathroom.

Styles, materials, lighting, and color

Modern design has allowed the bathroom to stop being the coldest-looking room in the home. Nowadays, comfort and beauty join forces to create any type of atmosphere or decorative style that you could want in a bathroom: minimalist, rustic, classical... The latest trends also enable you to achieve cutting-edge bathrooms that can become personal and unique with the addition of a few small details.

The combination of traditional materials like glass and tiles with more modern ones like porcelain and aluminum make it possible to create a room that is classical and heterodox at the same time. It is not only the materials that are important, however. Lighting and your choice of colors will add the finishing touches to the decoration of your bathroom.

Styles

Materials

© José Luis Hausmann

Lighting and color

Styles

When it comes to decorating a bathroom, it is vital to be clear about the style you want. This is the only way to achieve that personal touch that makes it unique and unmistakable.

There is a wide range of possible decorative styles, but none is better than the others. These days, there are no hard and fast rules. The most usual option consists of a combination of classical elements with more innovative features.

You can also have a rustic bathroom, characterized by an atmosphere that is in contact with nature. In contrast, a bathroom in an urban style will be marked by orderliness, sobriety and modernity in its lines, while a romantic bathroom will make use of classical elements and materials, embellished by soft lines and pastel colors, while a more dynamic bathroom that reflects the modern lifestyle will place the emphasis on taking full advantage of the space, without forsaking design criteria.

Choosing a classical decoration means opting for soft lines. In contrast, the modern style is characterized by its bold lines.

Minimalist bathrooms

© Margherita Spilluttini

This is the predominant style at the moment. Its basic premise is the avoidance of any excess of complements and unnecessary adornments. The motto of minimalist designers is "less is more", and they live up to this by eliminating any useless elements from a room so that it is governed by functional priorities. In this case, it is vital to have clear ideas about the space available in order to decide which elements are really necessary.

This type of decoration is dominated by pure and simple lines, which are used to both mark out the space and exploit its possibilities to the utmost. Color must also be taken into account. The minimalist style needs a totally unbroken monochrome on the walls, and this will subsequently be complemented by the furniture and decorative elements that will give your bathroom its final form. Use soft colors, especially white and cream, as these will supply the relaxed atmosphere needed in this type of room. In short, minimalist decoration tries to do away with anything that is superfluous.

© Nuria Fuentes

Minimalism is strongly influenced by
Oriental art, especially that of Japan.

© Nuria Fuentes

This bathroom is made up of basic
elements, while decorative details with
no useful purpose have been banished.

Minimalism is becoming popular
in the decoration of bathrooms
and this results in simple,
elegant spaces.

© Markus Tomaselli Rataplan

The use of color is very important. Contrasts are sought between the bathroom equipment and the color of the floor, walls and ceiling.

Romantic bathrooms

Despite the new styles, designs and materials that may crop up, some things never go out of fashion. There are people who want to go on opting for more classical decoration, in a style that defies new trends to remain relevant. The classical or romantic style is characterized by its sobriety, elegance and sophistication. This effect requires the use of more traditional furniture and complements, without resort to any more innovative options. Antique furniture is the most appropriate, especially if it is made of wood.

The romantic style seeks beauty and harmony in furniture by means of complements, colors and lighting. There is a preponderance of pale and pastel colors, which give a bathroom a touch of delicacy that cannot be achieved with more modern decoration. Using this range of colors, you will obtain greater luminosity, which is essential if your bathroom is lacking in natural light. Finally, it must be taken into account that the correct application of even the most trivial decorative details takes on an overriding importance. A few small personal touches (scented candles, a plant…) will endow your bathroom with character.

© José Luis Hausmann

© José Luis Hausmann

In this decorative style, soft colors are also predominant on the towels and drapes.

© José Luis Hausmann

Materials

The use of a particular material will set off the decorative style that you have selected for your bathroom. Your choice will depend on your preferences and, obviously, the budget at your disposal. You might find a material that is visually attractive but is also very difficult to look after. Similarly, an extremely cheap material may turn out expensive in the long run as may not be sufficiently water-resistant. The best solution is to find a balance between the price, resistance and ease of installation and maintenance.

The choice of a material will also depend on the size of the bathroom. In a big bathroom, it is very common for some of the walls to be totally or partially covered with mirrors. If you combine them with marble, you will add a modern touch to your bathroom. In contrast, you can opt for any materials for the walls of a small bathroom, except for wallpaper. Tiles are obligatory in the shower area, as they are the material most resistant to contact with the water, although in recent years the use of stone has become more widespread.

The use of glass, tiles or marble depend on your personal taste, but they are all appropriate for a bathroom.

© Duravit

© José Luis Hausmann

Glass

Glass is an underrated material that is a key ingredient for giving a bathroom a touch of distinction, regardless of its size and the style you have chosen. The primary glass object in a bathroom is the mirror. Large or small, framed or unframed—all options are good ones. The best idea is to complement them with halogen lamps, as these emit a clean light that prevents unappealing shadows from falling on your face.

Another glass element that is found in a bathroom is the partition. These days, transparent glass is most often used (as it enhances the visual sensation of depth), having been first tempered to make it much safer, as in this way it will not shatter into pieces if the screen breaks.

Finally, we must not forget the glass in windows. Large windows are an unbeatable source of natural light that will add a great deal of warmth to your bathroom. However, if your window is small, the glass will basically serve a decorative function and the light will have to be reinforced by artificial illumination.

© Nuria Fuentes

© Nuria Fuentes

Metal

Metal is one of the predominant elements in the decorative complements for a bathroom.

This is one of the traditional materials for bathrooms. It never goes out of fashion and can be used for all types of styles. In fact, it could be said that it is one of the few materials that are indispensable in a bathroom. Faucets and a good many decorative complements are made out of metal. Although it is true that metal is only used in small flourishes, it is, as we noted above, impossible to imagine a bathroom without its presence.

Metal can also be seen on mirrors, as a frame, and on screens by the bathtub or shower (in this case, the type of metal most frequently used is aluminum).

© Nuria Fuentes

Mosaic

This has been used practically since the 4th century BC and it is still commonly found on the walls and floors of bathrooms, on account of its many virtues. It has a natural appearance, is long-lasting and very easy to clean. Furthermore, it is perfect for rooms that are very busy, it bears up well to contact with water and it is very resistant. Mosaic offers many design possibilities and is usually installed in such a way that it depicts a form or creates a geometric motif, so a combination of colors, shapes and textures can come in very useful. It can also be combined with other materials, such as concrete and tiles, which enables it to be applied to curved surfaces, unlike many other materials.

As we have seen, the decorative possibilities are enormous. It is easy to find mosaics that suit your tastes, but before you make a final decision, you must consider where you are going to install it, in order to be able to choose the type of mosaic best suited to your requirements. In a bathroom, it is advisable to opt for mosaics that are non-slip and resistant to damp, as they will be in constant contact with water.

Stone

Stone is rough-looking and represents contact with nature; it is therefore predominant in bathrooms in a rustic style. It is one of the few materials suitable for both floors and cladding, while its forms, finishing and textures are practically unlimited. All types of stone are susceptible to breakages, so it is best to call in a specialist to install it. The stones that are most commonly found in bathrooms are marble, slate and granite. Marble gives a bathroom a more sophisticated look, although it needs more upkeep than tiles. It comes in a huge variety of textures, designs and colors. It is usually more expensive than other options, with the exception of granite.

Slate is much cheaper than both marble and granite. Its main advantage is that it is much easier to maintain. It is notable for its great resistance and is appropriate for more modern-looking bathrooms. Its range of colors is limited and tends toward the dark side, but it can be combined with a border of pale-colored tiles to give it greater luminosity. As for granite, it should be noted that it not only resists water but can also withstand the use of chemical products. Its texture must be rugged, otherwise it will be slippery.

© José Luis Hausmann

© José Luis Hausmann

The most popular finish for stone is a polish that provides sheen and bestows elegance on a bathroom.

NO

- To the bathroom mirror with no halogen lamps.
- To the excessive use of metal in the bathroom, as it is a cold material.
- To small tiles on large walls, and vice versa.
- Stone is a fragile material, so it is best not to install it yourself.

YES

- To glass as an indispensable element in your bathroom: it contributes elegance.
- To metal faucets. They do not rust after exposure to water.
- To tiles. They are impermeable and easy to clean.
- To stones with a rugged texture, to prevent slipping.

Lighting and color

A bathroom needs to be well-lit and, as we have mentioned above, light bulbs that complement the mirror and the washbasin area are the most important ones in the entire room. Halogen lamps are very appropriate, particularly if they are put along the sides of the mirror, as the light they produce is clean and free of shadows and irritating glare. It must also be remembered that a bathroom needs a more general light, in the form of a flush-fitting ceiling lamp with matt light bulbs or wall lamps with incandescent bulbs.

One final point: it is not advisable to put sockets and switches close to water. If there is no alternative, the installation must be undertaken by a qualified electrician.

As regards color, you must use shades that suggest warmth and hygiene at the same time. The most common colors are pastels, along with white and cream. Although dark colors should be avoided, as they are very cold, pastel shades of blue, green and gray are also suitable.

A specific light for shelves gives a bathroom a touch of distinction. This light should be clear and bright.

© José Luis Hausmann

© José Luis Hausmann

© José Luis Hausmann

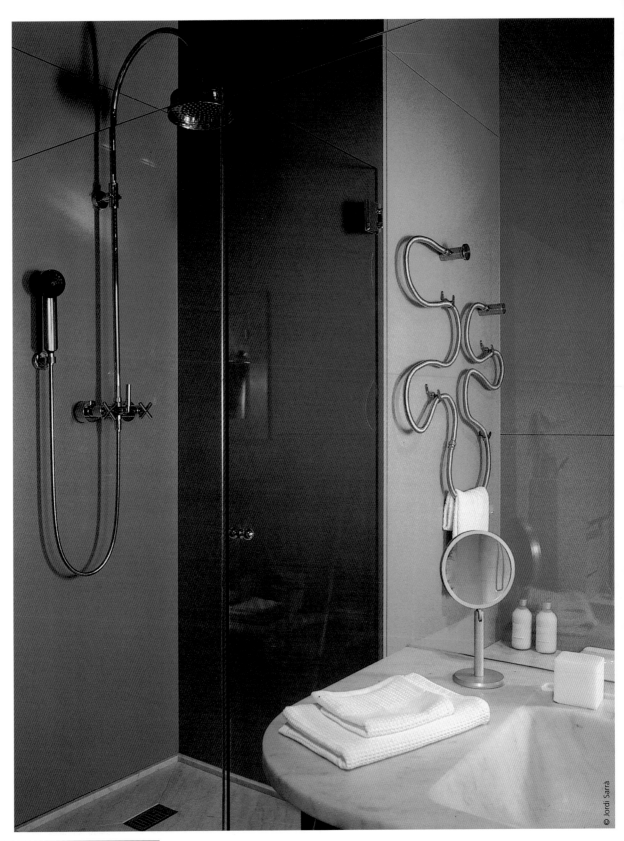

© Jordi Sarrà

© Jordi Sarrà

© Jordi Sarrà

© Pep Escoda

© Jordi Sarrà

© Jordi Sarrà

© Jordi Sarrà

Bathroom equipment and accessories

Thirty years ago nobody would have imagined that bathrooms would take on the importance that they have nowadays. At that time no attempts were made to combine materials and colors, and a bathroom would be almost entirely the same color as the washbasin and bidet. It was a simple room with few decorative elements and its only function was to satisfy the requirements of personal hygiene. It has now become a space in which we seek to relax after a long day at work and so its decoration needs to conform to our tastes and evoke a welcoming atmosphere, while still being functional.

There are now thousands of fittings and complements to choose from, in various colors and designs. None is better than the others: if they are chosen with care, they can all add a personal touch to your bathroom.

Bathtubs

Showers

Washbasins and toilets

Accessories

© Jose Luis Hausmann

Bathtubs

Whether you opt for a bathtub or a shower, it has to provide the required degree of hygiene and relaxation. Why choose a bathtub? Because there is enough space available to allow you to install it and, moreover, because you consider bath time as the ideal opportunity to forget about your worries. A bathtub full of hot water, with a candle to give a touch of warmth, will allow you to fully enjoy the therapeutic effects of water.

Some bathtubs maintain the heat of the water better than others, on account of the material with which they are made. Most of the bathtubs on the market are made of stainless steel and marble. These are cold, expensive materials that rapidly lower water temperature, but they are also long-lasting. Another option is to install a hard-wood bathtub. Wood is also an expensive material but it is warmer to the touch and conserves heat efficiently. Finally, you could go for a copper bathtub, which is the most popular of all. It is a cold material, but it is the cheapest and it is easy to look after.

The combination of a bath and a shower in the same corner makes it possible to take full advantage of the space.

© Andrée Putman for Hoesch Design

© Norman Foster for Hoesch Design

There is a wide range of models of bathtubs. Any corner can be suitable to install one, as they come in shapes that adapt to almost all possibilities.

When cleaning a bathtub, it is best not to use products with ammonia. Abrasive substances are to be avoided.

© Eugenia Uhl

© David Loftus

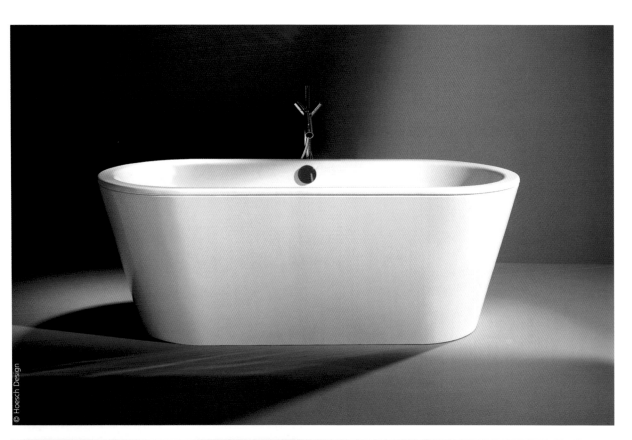

Showers

People who decide to install a shower rather than a bathtub do so for two basic reasons: firstly, lack of time to take a bath and, secondly, and most importantly, restrictions on space. Showers are suited to bathrooms integrated into a bedroom because these are normally small spaces.

As we have said, the space at our disposal is usually limited, although these days this does not pose a problem. Modern industrial design has provided us with an enormous variety of shower trays, cubicles, screens and accessories that can be combined to extend the offer even further. These days there are alternatives to single showers: double showers can also be found. These are usually rectangular, but they also come in much more flexible round models.

The size of the shower try varies according to the space available. Apart from the nozzle, which is set at the top of the shower, there is a possibility of inserting side spouts that send jets of water on to the body.

If you have sufficient space, a corner
shower enables you to install
a double tray.

© Duravit

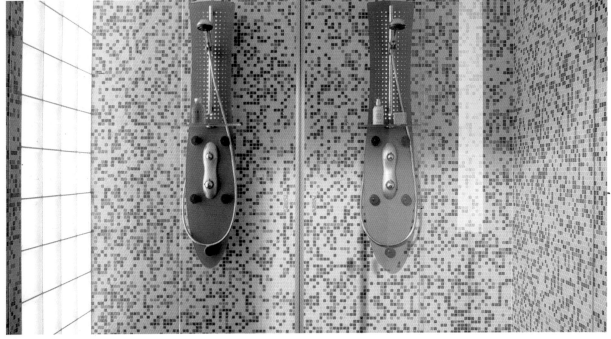

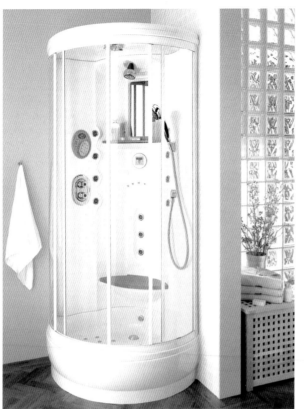

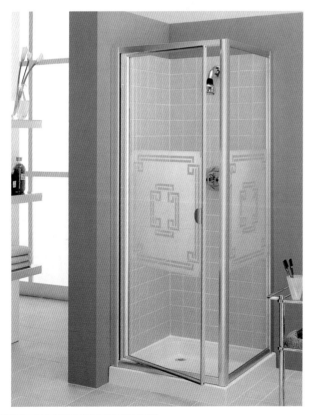

© Dornbracht

© Flaminia

© Duravit

© Davide Vercelli for Ritmonio

Washbasins

Design has reached even the fittings in a bathroom. Washbasins are indispensable features that are being increasingly adapted to modern trends.

Not all washbasins are alike. The most widely used material is marble; although it is expensive, it is usually recommended by experts because it is very resistant and easy to clean. Although marble washbasins are traditional favorites, it is easy to find new models that are gradually creating a niche in the market. Washbasins in glass, wood and porcelain have emerged, and these give a bathroom a modern touch. These materials need to be handled with care as they are very fragile and can get scratched.

The classic washbasin is oval, but round, rectangular and square models are more popular today.

Finally, the installation of a washbasin is not complete without the right faucets. These have also changed with the times and are the ideal complement to an attractively designed washbasin.

The classic porcelain washbasin is losing ground to models made of wood, porcelain and glass.

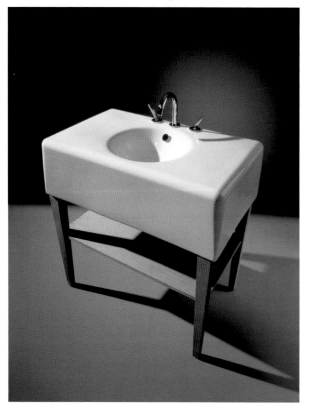

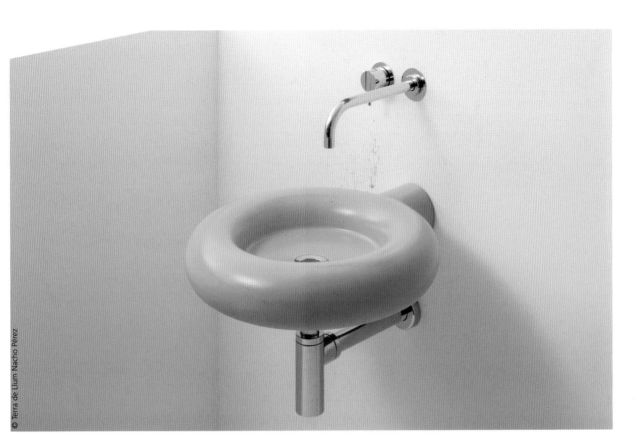

© Roberto Constantini

© Roberto Constantini

© Roberto Constantini

© Roberto Constantini

© Flaminia

Toilets

As in the case of the washbasin, design has totally transformed the concept that we had until recently of toilets. Just a few years ago, all that was required of a toilet was to fulfill its function. Nowadays, a degree of esthetic harmony is also desired, in order to combine perfectly with the style of the bathroom and its decoration. The toilet and bidet are companions that come in a wide range of shapes, styles and colors. There are two types of toilets: the monoblock and the wall-mounted. The former is complete, i.e., it touches the floor and is joined to it by means of a "base" or "column". This is the most common model and it is characterized by a cistern attached to the bowl. The main advantage of this model is its low noise level.

The other type is the wall-mounted toilet. This is fixed to the wall (which has to be sufficiently solid) and hangs in the air without touching the floor. The main advantages of this model are that it facilitates the cleaning of the surrounding area and is visually interesting.

If you opt for a wall-mounted toilet, you will need sufficient space behind the wall or to the side to install the cistern.

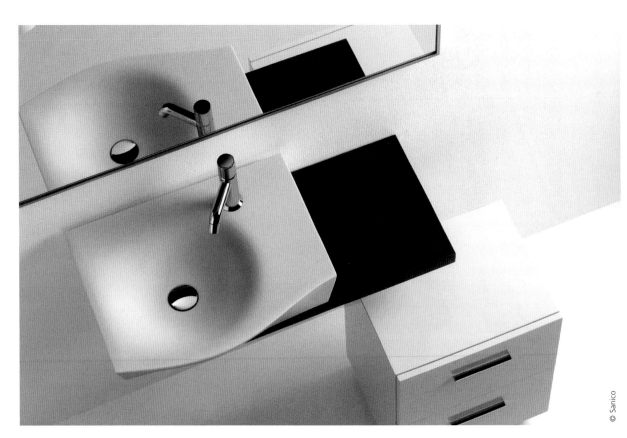

© Sanico

Both the classical and modern styles
are good options—what is important
is to complement a toilet with the
right details.

© Flaminia

Accessories

ere begins the last phase of the decoration of your bathroom. You have decided on a decorative style in accordance with the space available; you have chosen the materials for the ceiling, floor and walls; you have bought the kitchen equipment you need and all you need to do now is to complement it with those details that will give it a distinctive look.

Drapes for the windows; closets, whether big or small, fitted with the washbasin, made to measure and with rollers; mirrors, with or without frames; towel rails that complement both each other and the faucets; soap trays; jars for toothbrushes…

These are the elements that add personality to a bathroom, and so they are just as important as the choice of the bathroom equipment.

It is important to use elements that combine with each other. This will allow you to bestow elegance on your bathroom.

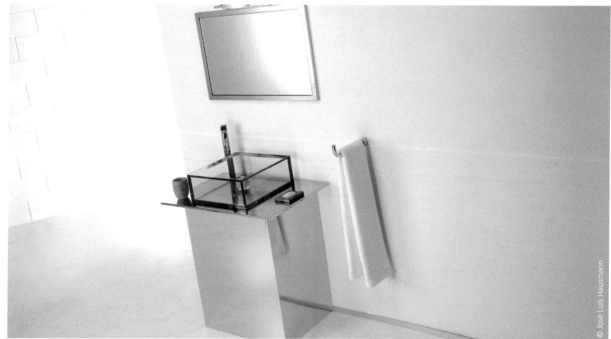

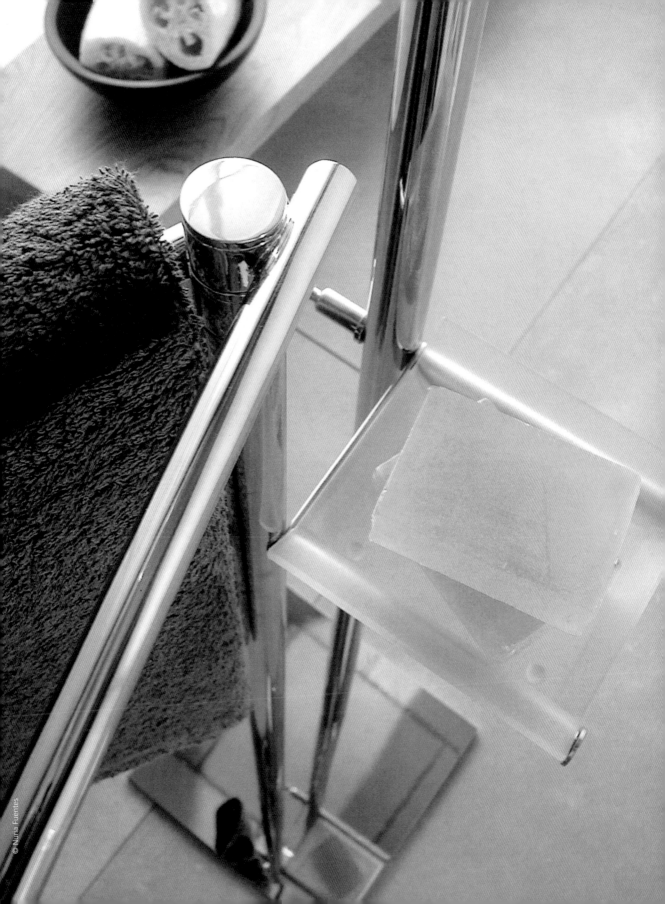

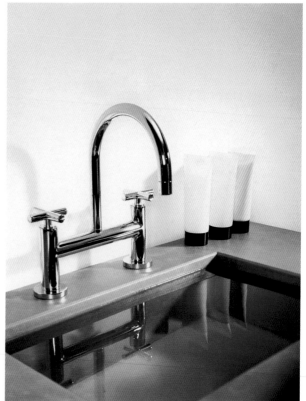

© Dornbracht

© Trentino

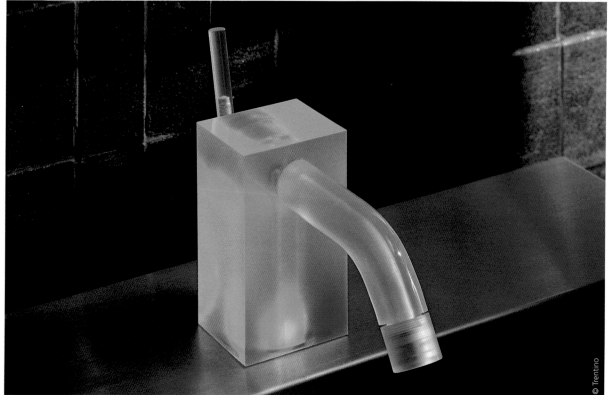

© Trentino

© Peter Jamieson for Ritmonio

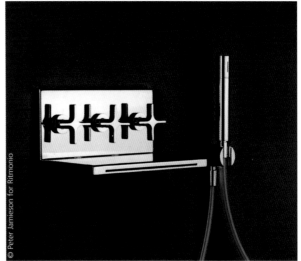

© Peter Jamieson for Ritmonio

© Peter Jamieson for Ritmonio

© Peter Jamieson for Ritmonio

© Davide Vercelli for Ritmonio

© Davide Vercelli for Ritmonio

Faucets are the ideal complement for a washbasin. The faucets and accessories currently available adapt to modern design by means of their innovative shapes and sizes.

© Falper

© Sanico

© Sanico

© Sanico

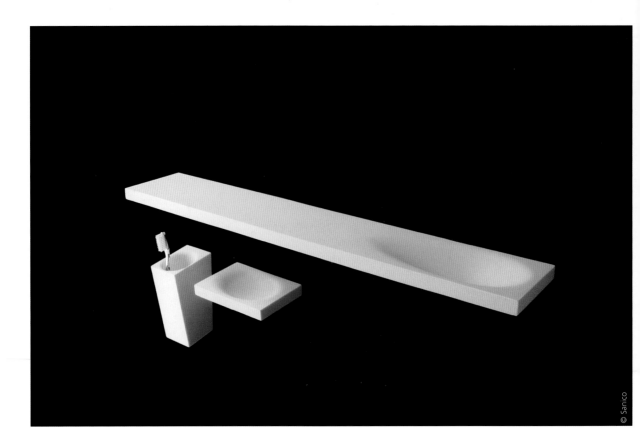

Aim for simplicity in the lines to avoid overwhelming your bathroom. White and cream are the most appropriate colors for this type of complement.

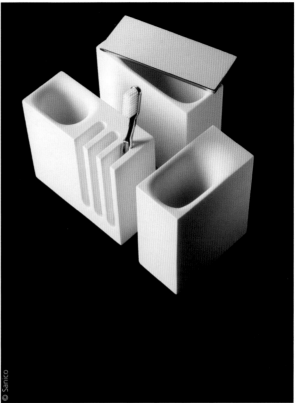

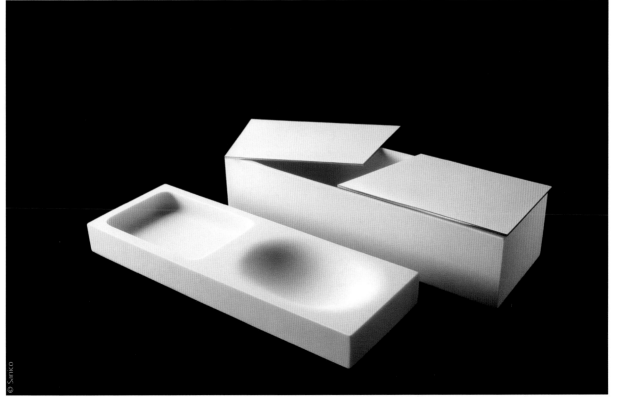

© Duravit

Design has also reached towel rails, allowing them to add an original flourish to a bathroom with a few simple geometric forms.

© Dornbracht

© Núria Fuentes

Made-to-measure closets on rollers are becoming increasingly popular, as they make it easier to keep a bathroom clean and tidy.

The object is to take full advantage of the available space. Simple objects can give a bathroom a sophisticated look, without any unnecessary ornamentation.

© Sanico

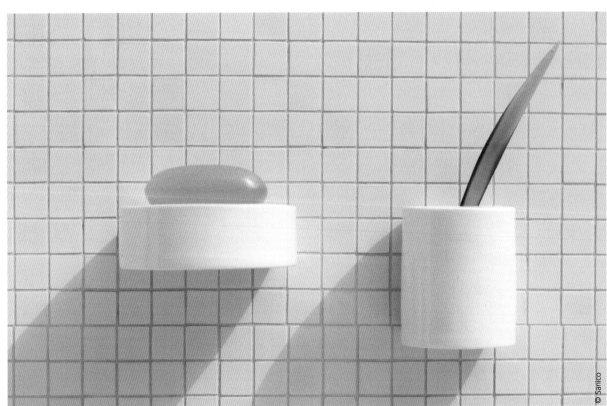

© Sanico

The combination of complements can embrace even the most insignificant objects.

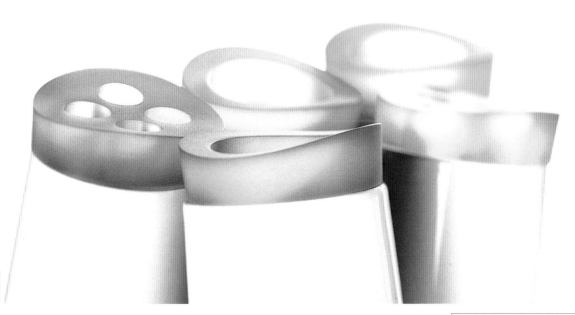

Kitchens

Types of kitchens
Styles
Storage
Accessories

Types of kitchens

As in the case of bathrooms, modern design has also influenced the decoration of today's kitchens and enabled them to combine functionality with beauty. Design features can enable you to create a comfortable space, regardless of the size of your kitchen, as they can allow you to work without obstacles.

You must be absolutely clear about the elements you plan to put in your kitchen. If it is sufficiently big, you can consider the possibility of adding a table and some chairs, or even your washing machine, as this will make your domestic chores easier.

Today's kitchens draw on a host of electrical devices. This makes the lighting plan a key factor—and make sure you are generous when it comes to installing plugs and switches.

Closed kitchens

Open kitchens

Kitchen islands

© Montse Garriga

Closed kitchens

An enclosed, independent kitchen prevents smoke and cooking smells from invading the rest of the home. To allow smoke to disperse rapidly, it is advisable to fit a window in the kitchen to encourage rapid ventilation.

In an enclosed space, however, lighting takes on a primordial importance. The kitchen is a place for working and so it requires appropriate lighting that is as "clean" as possible. The best option for the work areas would be fitted fluorescent tubes, which are normally quite cheap. The ideal place to put them is above or in front of the work area: if they are set behind your back, irritating shadows will appear.

Finally, do not keep utensils that you may never use in the kitchen: this room should be supremely functional.

Made-to-measure closets and a series of shelves will help you keep your kitchen utensils in order, while adding a modern touch to the room.

Extractor hoods allow smoke to escape the cooking process.

Open kitchens

Open kitchens are becoming increasingly common. As in closed ones, or even more so, ventilation is essential to get rid of smoke and unpleasant smells. As we have seen, you must be clear about the space you have available before subsequently dividing it into three areas: one for storage, one for preparation and one for cooking. These three areas usually form an L or a U, which is the most frequent layout for modern kitchens.

The storage area is where the ingredients needed for cooking are kept. The preparation area will contain the sink and will be set close to the fridge. Finally, the cooking area will house the cooker and the utensils needed to conjure up meals.

As regards lighting, an open kitchen will probably have the advantage of a source of sunlight. If this is not the case, the installation of spotlights or fluorescent tubes will provide the light you need to work. If you have space for a table and a few chairs for everyday use, an overhead lamp will help to create a differentiated space within a single room.

© Binova

Large windows can not only enhance
lighting but also help to separate spaces.

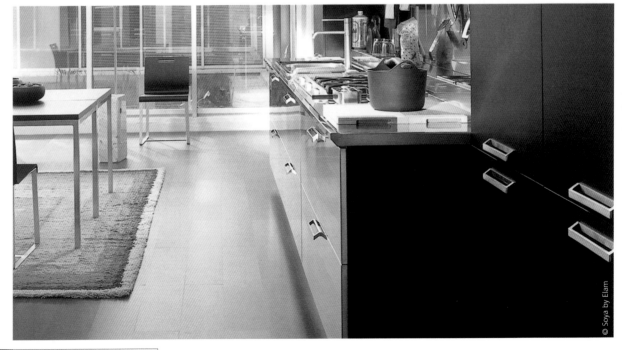

© Soya by Elam

Kitchen islands

Functionality and design: these are the objectives pursued by a modern kitchen. One good way of fulfilling these aims is by installing an island that can serve various functions: as a central space in the kitchen (if it also includes the cooker), as a space for preparing dough or cutting food, or simply as a dining table.

Placing an island in the center of your kitchen will add an original touch to the decoration. Its height and measurements will depend on the space available. It has to be sufficiently far from the rest of the furniture and equipment to allow closet doors to open comfortably and provide enough space to move around the work area in freedom.

The closets on your island will make it possible to take full advantage of the space. One good option is extractable shelves that allow you to make use of corners. Large kitchen utensils can be stored in the bigger drawers. Finally, the most commonly found islands have tops with laminated tiles or ceramics.

© Berloni Cucine

Installing a kitchen on an island will help you save space in the rest of the room.

© Elmar Cucine

Opting for a worktop and furniture in
the same style as the rest of the kitchen
will harmonize the decoration.

The island can also be a quiet place where children can do their homework close to their parents.

A lamp will be an appropriate complement and will provide the light that we need in this area.

Styles

A kitchen is highly functional by nature. Nevertheless, its decoration must not be neglected. Modern design allows us to create highly innovative and visually striking kitchens without losing one iota of functionality. It is important for the personal style and tastes of the occupant to hold sway in a kitchen. Give it that unique touch that will make it different from all other kitchens.

There are countless decorative options on offer, but three styles are currently predominant: minimalism, which seeks to take the maximum advantage of space by eliminating any superfluous element, without neglecting design criteria; the urban style, which adapts to modern life and is primarily governed by order and functionality; and the rustic style, which bases its decoration on a more classical note, in touch with nature.

Minimalist kitchens

Urban kitchens

Rustic kitchens

© Bulthaup

Minimalist kitchens

These days, many people have opted to forsake the classical style that until recently dominated the decoration of most homes. Design has obviously also reached the kitchen, and minimalism is gradually having a greater impact. This style rejects all unnecessary complements, is characterized by its pure, simple lines and draws on simple furniture, albeit endowed with charm. In this case, the important thing is to take full advantage of the space, without overloading a kitchen with any superfluous features. The materials and complements are what make these kitchens special and different.

As regards colors, there is a predominance of pale colors like white and cream, as they heighten luminosity and look hygienic. With respect to materials, wood complemented by a few steel or aluminum elements is unbeatable in visual terms. Finally, remember that the complements you choose (steel racks that fit in a corner, small shelves, etc.) will endow your kitchen with personality.

Order is a basic requirement in a modern kitchen, so designers have created a wide range of closets to keep all kinds of utensils.

© Boffi

© Binova

Lighting needs to be clear and bright, to
allow you to work without having to
strain your eyes.

The use of various shades of wood has
extremely attractive results in a kitchen.

© Elmar Cucine

© Soya by Elam

Glass is also a good complement, because it contrasts with furniture made of opaque materials.

<table>
<tr><td>

NO

• To any excess of electrical devices and complements on the worktop, as these will overload the space unnecessarily.

• To any unnecessary furniture in the kitchen, as this will end up becoming an obstacle and will reduce the functionality of the kitchen.

</td><td>

YES

• To the installation of closets of different sizes, as they will allow you to store your kitchen utensils.

• To pale colors combined with steel and aluminum, as they enhance luminosity.

</td></tr>
</table>

Urban kitchens

These days it is normal for both the man and woman of a household to go out and work, and this has led them to share the domestic chores. Moreover, the limits on the time we can spend at home means that we prefer spaces that are pleasant, comfortable, functional and, in the case of kitchens, very practical.

The urban style is ideally suited to this search for functionality inherent to the modern lifestyle. In an urban kitchen, order is the key and it is vital to have the necessary space to cook in comfort.

As we have said, order is primordial and, to achieve this, designers have come up with closets in all shapes and sizes that can be put in any nook or cranny and are reasonably priced. Simple, pure lines predominate, in keeping with a room where hygiene is of crucial importance.In short, the fact that you are seeking functionality for your kitchen does not preclude modern design and the latest trends.

Large, small, with drawers, closets come in all sorts of forms that can successfully make your kitchen as practical as possible.

The resistant qualities of wood and aluminum make them materials well suited to kitchens.

© Soya by Elam

© Miele

© Berloni Cucine

Sketch

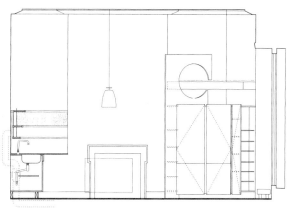

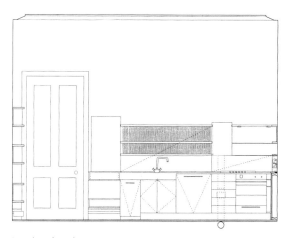

Interior elevation

© Jonathan Pile

Rustic kitchens

I f you want your kitchen to be simple, comfortable and in contact with nature, the ideal option would be decoration in a rustic style.

This would be dominated by dark furniture, giving a key role to the lighting and layout to avoid making the room seem excessively small. The combination of materials will help achieve the comfortable setting you seek, and their choice will depend on the budget at your disposal. The most commonly used material is wood, whether solid, laminated or plywood. It is also important to choose the right complements. Iron, clay and tiles will give you that warm, cozy finish so typical of kitchens in this style.

As for cladding, the walls are generally covered with brick or stone, although they are also usually painted in the same range of colors used in the rest of the kitchen. The important thing is to ensure that there is an overall harmony that allows us to combine design and functionality.

Earthy colors, black, silver and gold are the colors that predominate in this type of kitchen.

Painted ceramics, steel and macramé are
ideal complements.

Islands are not usually found in this
decorative style. The central space in
this type of kitchen is usually given
over to a dining table.

Sketch

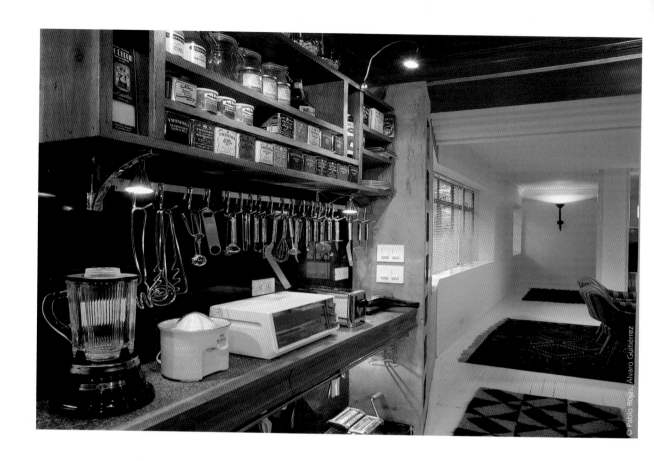

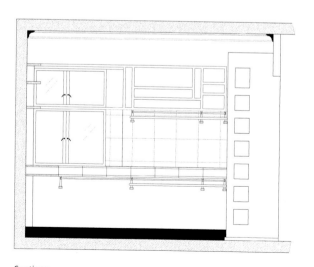

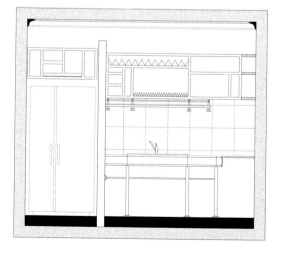

Sections

Storage

The kitchen is the room in which we need the most utensils and, therefore, the one that requires the most storage facilities.

The first thing to take into account is that you must not pile up your utensils and that you must keep everything within easy reach, ready for the moment when they may be required. Modern closets now usually incorporate revolving shelves. This means that the items in the corners are not overlooked. Another possibility is fitted closets, made to measure for a particular place to store anything from bottles to the products used to clean the kitchen.

The priorities are to aim for comfort and make your work easier. The cooker should be set between the fridge and the sink, because in this way you will have the ingredients for your meals on one side and the space for leaving and cleaning the utensils you use on the other. Moreover, it is essential that there is a closet especially designed for pots and pans close to the cooker.

Lamps fitted into furniture offer a good means for improving the lighting in the work areas.

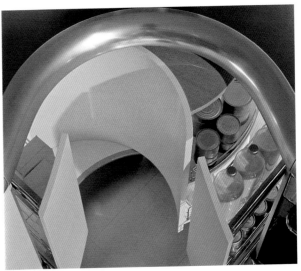

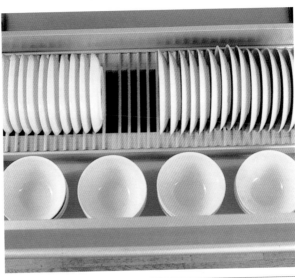

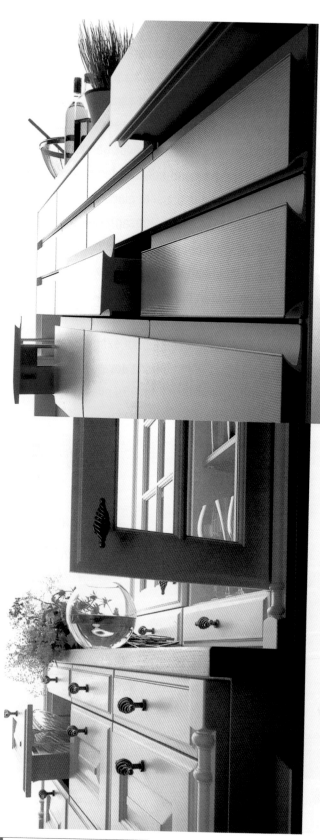

Accessories

We have reached the end. All that remains is to give the final touches to your kitchen by adding small decorative details. These complements must be practical, so you should avoid all useless accessories.

The sink is one of the most important elements. To give it its own personality, the best option is a shape that until recently was highly unusual (round or oval). The ideal complement? A modern faucet unit fitted into its upper surface. We have mentioned the great variety of closets currently on the market. Handles may seem elements of little importance, but they are accessories with simple lines that also help to create a distinctive style.

Small display cases for keeping crockery; shelve with fitted lights that pick out a decorative element; aluminum racks for a variety of utensils, and made-to-measure furniture. Tthese are the practical but decorative complements that will allow you to satisfy the two essential requirements of your kitchen: design and functionality.

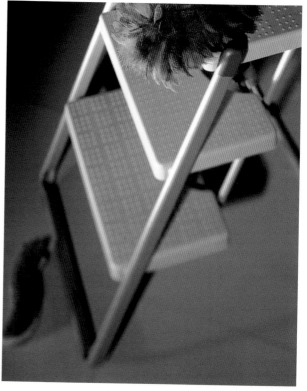

Aluminum sinks are the most appropriate for kitchens, because they resist the passing of time most effectively.

© Montse Garriga

Elements which at first sight may seem insignificant can also be relevant. The smallest detail plays a part in achieving the kitchen you are searching for.

© Elmar Cucine

NO

• To an excess of decorative complements that serve no useful purpose and get in the way.
• To electrical devices on the worktop, as they will only take up space.

YES

• To books and dried plants for decoration. They add a personal touch and bring a kitchen close to nature.
• To steel and metal on the handles of closets, because the contrast in materials usually looks very elegant.